Preface

The one-hundred year anniversary of the driving of the golden (or iron) spike which occurs May 10, 1969, is both occasion for national celebration and for some degree of regret.

On May 10, 1869, the Atlantic and Pacific coasts of this nation were united by iron rail. The alternative transportation methods of the day: stagecoach, Conestoga wagon, clipper ship, steamship, and hand cart left much to be desired as to comfort, speed, safety, and degree of utility.

It is difficult to realize in this thoroughly highway-oriented era what a difference the completion of the overland route made. A trip from the East to West Coast that once required months was reduced to days.

The irony of the present-day situation is that the Centennial of the completion of the nation's first transcontinental railroad route will also nearly come close to being the terminal date of the expiration of transcontinental passenger train travel. It may very well be that the next five years will bring the very last run of any transcontinental train whatsoever.

It has therefore been exceptionally difficult to figure out precisely how to pitch the artistic content of the commemorative exhibit that has been devised to celebrate the culmination of the nation's constructive efforts that is being placed before you. The means to accomplish such an exhibit are not lacking, nor are they unknown to the authors of this show. Glass plate negatives of many of the great pioneer western photographers exist literally by the ton and are proudly and carefully preserved by a wide variety of custodial institutions. The Golden Era of railroading coincides precisely with the golden era of photography. For this reason, the exhibit at hand had to be expressed in the medium of photography. And what better medium? The efforts of A. J. Russell, C. R. Savage, F. J. Haynes, W. H. Jackson, H. H. Buchwalter, L. C. McClure, Asahel Curtis, and J. E. Stimson represent the best work done during what might be well described as the ponderous period of photography. A show representing the original efforts of any one of these pioneer photographers could be presented from *the original negatives* still in existence and would be of stunning artistic effect. Each photographer was a master of his particular time, place and era. It would be entirely feasible, and artistically beneficial, to have an exhibit of 300 L. C. McClure photographs in wallboard size enlargements of the building of the Denver, Northwestern & Pacific Railway in Colorado as it would be to present a like cross-section of the efforts of F. Jay Haynes in depicting the westward progress of the Northern Pacific Railway across the State of Montana.

It might be noted that as the size of the *impedimenta* required became less that a huge amateur bevy of photographers arose that were anxious and, what is more to the point, highly capable, of recording the interesting visual bill-of-fare that is afforded by the American railway scene. Certainly, one would be forced to acknowledge the efforts of Fred Jukes, J. Foster Adams, H. H. Arey, A. W. Johnson, Gerald M. Best,

Donald Duke, Lucius Beebe, Charles M. Clegg, Roland Collons, S. R. Wood, Otto Perry, Douglas C. Wornom, James Ehernberger, R. H. Kindig, and Richard Steinheimer to name only a few of the more technically skillful railroad buffs who have specialized in the railroad scene as it exists west of the Mississippi River. It might be noted that many of the efforts of the pioneer moderns were made despite the heartfelt resistance of the railroad companies whose action they wished to photograph. The same companies, now having depleted their files of the "obsolete" material they once used to maintain, are now coming back to the same buffs, whom they were formerly so careful to usher off their premises, for equivalents of the same materials that they had discarded.

We have therefore elected the somewhat odd-ball approach of utilizing modern photographs to depict aspects of railroading that were current when Jay Gould was still the terror of Wall Street. The most wondrous aspect of the American railroad industry is that its practices, structural personifications, and equipment have not basically changed since the first steam railroad was built in this country in 1829.

Let the author of this book speak both from his heart and from his own personal knowledge and observation of American railroads since that day in September, 1933, when he first raised a Box-Brownie No. 2 at a railroad locomotive. Since that totally unremarkable date will pass by unnoticed by posterity, it seems worthy to mention that he has since photographed some 25,000 railroad subjects single-handed and acquired in one way or another 65,000 negatives made by other individuals. There are few industries more photogenic than a railroad and the complexities of making a truly representative group of photographs of the paraphernalia of even one railroad are beyond belief. To cite but one example, the author has been attempting to photograph all remaining structures on the former Erie and Lackawanna railroads west from Hoboken, N. J. to Susquehanna, Pennsylvania and to Stroudsburg, Pennsylvania, respectively. To date, he has visited over 188 different locations and the task is still only about three-quarters complete!

Therefore, little of the retrospective aspects of railroading will be included between the covers of this book. Original prints of the work of Russell, Jackson and others are included in plenty in the show itself, but not many have been included in this catalog as a number of books have currently been published that contain the work of the pioneer photographers *in extenso.*

Two major efforts have been made in the selection for the show and for this catalog. The first is to show the railroad in its environment. On the western transcontinental railroads, rugged topography is the dominant characteristic and an effort has been made to emphasize this all-important factor. Another environmental factor of importance is climate. Railroads are truly twenty-four-hour-a-day, allweather operations of astounding reliability, and this is nowhere better exemplified than in those operations of the roads that extend singly, or in combination, from the Missouri and Mississippi Rivers to the Pacific Coast.

The second attempt is to demonstrate visually that one railroad is different than another. In the steam era, this was easier than it has since become. One could look at a locomotive, car, or station, and almost immediately recognize its provenance. The diesel locomotive, the standard-design box car, and the stainless steel coach have done much to obliterate the distinction of the mechanical idiosyncracies of the various carriers. The rural station is now, particularly in the West, conspicuous by its absence. Replacement of the pioneer structures (and *one* station was all that many communities have ever had), if made at all, has been by Bailey buildings of great simplicity and ingenuity but of no architectural distinction.

A minor effort has been made to illustrate what might be termed railroad archaeology. Many of the pioneer lines (though but one of the transcontinentals, the Colorado Midland) have been abandoned. Further abandonments would seem to be both desirable and enlightened as consolidation of formerly independent operations ensues. The author would hope that he has indicated that, even when the trains and tracks have vanished, there is often much left to record.

As previously indicated, available historical photographs employed are in limited number. A large portion of the modern-era ones are now historical — as indicated in the captions, many of the trains, particularly passenger trains, have made their last runs and many of the diesels have been replaced by larger and more powerful units. So in a real sense this is more or less of a historical coverage of the western railroad scene even though it might not appear to be so.

The author would like to acknowledge a special debt to a few of the many people involved in the assembly of this exhibit. Most of the copy work was done by Gammon Studios in Dallas. George Kincaid, of Dallas, furnished many of the enlarged prints. Slides were made by Mrs. Linda Lorenz of the Amon Carter Museum. The concept of the exhibit was that of Mr. Mitchell A. Wilder and his capable staff.

The individual firms, institutions and photographers are individually credited. To them, my gratitude is boundless, as without their efforts there would be no show.

Everett L. DeGolyer, Jr.

THE TRACK GOING BACK

Plate 1

Promontory, Utah, is now indeed a ghost town but here the last golden spike was driven on May 10, 1869, commemorating the joining of the rails of the Union Pacific and Southern Pacific railroads and, hence, the linking of the Atlantic and Pacific coasts at that point.

Promontory was on the main line until the construction of the Lucin cut-off over Great Salt Lake early in this century during the regime of E. H. Harriman. However, it was kept alive as a sparsely trafficked branch until it was abandoned in the early part of World War II.

Richard Steinheimer photograph

LAST SPIKE
COMPLETING FIRST
TRANSCONTINENTAL
RAILROAD
DRIVEN AT THIS POINT
MAY 10TH 1869

Plate 2

The Milwaukee Road was really a very old company, having been incorporated in Wisconsin as far back as May 5, 1863, as the Milwaukee & St. Paul Railway. On February 14, 1874, it became the Chicago, Milwaukee & St. Paul Railway, and enjoyed a long career of financial impeccability and fiscal probity in its original status as a foremost granger carrier.

Unfortunately, the urge to the Pacific set in about 1905, and what had been for years a blue chip became, over the next decades, 10,000 miles of legal nightmares, the denouement of which is still a question.

However, when this archetypical roundhouse pose was made, presumably about 1880, all portents were excellent for the company.

No. 529, "D. L. Bush", is one of the rarest birds, a Niles-built locomotive.

Photographer unknown
Everett L. DeGolyer, Jr. collection

Plate 3

The late Robert R. Young characterized the standard open-section Pullman sleeping cars as "rolling tenements", but the term would be more aptly applied to the two- and three-story bunk cars used on the Great Northern Railway during its westward march across the mountains and prairies in the late 1880s and early 1890s. These extremely high cars were provided with cables to prevent their capsizing when parked at windy locations and with platforms underneath for the more unwieldy belongings of the construction workers who resided in them.

Great Northern Railway photograph

Plate 4

First harbingers of the coming of the iron horse are the civil engineers, well in advance of the main construction gang, who ride forth and, if they are skilled in their calling, will elect the route with the least number of curves and gradients. This is a job for men who are strictly out-of-doors types.

On Chehalis Prairie, Washington. May, 1891. Northern Pacific Railroad.

Photographer unknown
DeGolyer Foundation Library

Plate 5

Then as now, blueprints are essential documents in any type of railroad construction activity. Printing still was the most easily performed by natural light, and apparatus, though crude, got the job done splendidly. Northern Pacific Railroad, Tacoma, Washington, mid 1880s.

BLUE PRINTING APPARATUS.

Plate 6

One of the most impressive of all construction sights after the 1880 period were the giant Bucyrus steam shovels, rail-mounted, which could chaw out cuts at a prodigious rate. These disgorged their loads of fill into four-wheeled dump cars pulled by dinky locomotives over temporary tracks which were, more often than not, narrow gauge. Needless to state, the additional weight of the rock levered way out on the boom required extra support bracing which we can see to the left of the body of the shovel.

These giant earth-moving devices are now scarce items indeed on most railroads, but in their time were among the most impressive units in the armamentarium of railroad contractors.

This big Bucyrus is hard at work on the Chicago, Milwaukee & Puget Sound Railway near Missoula, Mont. in 1907.

Montana State Historical Society photograph

Plate 7

Next in order behind the powder and earth-moving crews was the tie-laying gang. Modern practice (on the rare occasions when a new railroad line is built) is to lay track in panels with a crane, but in the old days, mechanization was elemental, labor cheap, and everything was done the hard way. Northern Pacific Railroad, State of Washington, 1891.

Plate 8

The first step in bridgebuilding was to drive piles for the footing. The topography in this case apparently did not permit the employment of the customary car-transported type of pile driver, so a small one was floated in on a long raft. Second crossing of Chehalis River, Northern Pacific, April 1891.

Photographer unknown
DeGolyer Foundation Library

Plate 9

Next step in bridge construction was the erection of falsework, upon which the main truss span would be supported until its final completion. The engineer of this early Northern Pacific construction train must have been a lion-hearted man as he eased his little American Standard type locomotive cautiously out upon the groaning timbers. First crossing of the Chehalis River, May 1891.

Photographer unknown
DeGolyer Foundation Library

Plate 10

This view is concrete evidence that there was much haste in the construction of the Union Pacific and that its track was in dire need of further manicuring even after the line had been opened to traffic. Indeed, the radical reconstruction of the original Overland route by E. H. Harriman in the 1890s and 1900s is one of the great epics of western railroading.

The scene is Hall's Fill above Granite Canyon.

Photographer unknown
Yale University Library

Plate 11

Some prodigious feats of construction occurred during the building of the Union Pacific. One of the true man-made wonders of the line was the massive timber trestle over Dale Creek, Wyoming, completed April 13, 1868. Eight years later, it was replaced by an iron structure, necessitated by the increasingly heavy locomotives employed on the line. The granite footings of the original bridge were utilized by the replacement. The wooden decking of the iron bridge caught fire from locomotive sparks in 1884, and the bridge was condemned the next year, although not replaced until 1890.

In 1900-1901, the line over Sherman Hill was relocated, and a new crossing made over Dale Creek by a fill.

The busy bridges-and-buildings gangs of the U.P. required only thirty working days to fabricate this huge structure, nearly 600 feet long and 125 feet high, which was largely fashioned of pine timbers brought in from Chicago.

A. J. Russell photograph
DeGolyer Foundation Library

Plate 12

One of the big items of traffic on the early Northern Pacific was coal. The company had it in abundance at its fields at Wilkeson, Newcastle and Carbondale, and was thus not only possessed of sufficient fuel for its own locomotives, but had sufficient to sell elsewhere.

This is an early view of the coal-loading facility at Tacoma, Washington, whereby the fuel could be discharged directly from the railroad cars into the holds of waiting sailing vessels.

Photographer unknown
DeGolyer Foundation Library

Plate 13

Reams of paper work accompany the construction of a railroad when literally thousands of men, machines, horses, tools and materials must all be accounted for. This early Northern Pacific accountant didn't even have an abacus to help out his computations, but he did, however, have a secretary. As is still usually the case in the railroad industry, the latter functionary is male.

Considering the time and place, and the exigencies of the profession, the accountant was no doubt a British national.

CONSTRUCTION DEP'T ACCOUNTING CLERK
ROOM 35.

Plate 14

The most joyful sight to be encountered on any western railroad was the pay car heaving into view on its monthly rounds. Checks were not a matter of clerical concern in those days; the miniscule wages by the company were dispensed in the form of cold cash and on the spot.

The garb of the paymaster's crew in this early Northern Pacific view suggests that, once the wages had been paid, they would be quite capable of repossessing the moneys in a quick game of faro.

Plate 15

A typical rendition of roundhouse activity is provided by the Union Pacific forces at Echo, Utah, presumably in the 1880s. All locomotives in the house on this day have pulled out into the sunshine and are flanked by their respective crews. The author finds it hard to believe that the photographer did not tip them off in advance — frock coats, vests, ties and hats were not everyday working togs for the railroad men of that day and time, and it is unlikely that that many of them had been attending church.

Photographer unknown
Everett L. DeGolyer, Jr. collection

Plate 16

Surely the windmill to end all windmills is this monster whose purpose in life was to keep filled the company's water tank at Laramie, Wyoming. In fact, its stature might entitle it to the appellation of wind engine. To quote photographer Russell, it was ". . . self-regulating, ingenious in construction, and durable, having never failed to supply the demands of the railroad."

The Laramie roundhouse and shops, in the background, are constructed durably of sandstone.

A. J. Russell photograph
DeGolyer Foundation Library

Plate 17

The Denver Union Station was constructed in the form shown in this photo in 1880. In 1894, a fire razed the center portion and required rebuilding of the roofs of the two wings. In 1914, an entirely new monumental central wing was erected, but the outlying wings of 1880 survive to this day.

Plate 18

It may not so appear to us now, but Canadian Pacific Railway No. 314, a Baldwin built Consolidation type, was a huge locomotive in 1889 when this photo was made somewhere in the Canadian Rockies.

The icy majesty of this mountain range supplies a superb backdrop to the coal sheds and locomotive.

THE HEAVY GRADE ENGINE, IN THE ROCKIES.

Plate 19

Joyful festivity is suggested by the view of Canadian
Pacific Railway No. 374, the first locomotive into
Vancouver, B.C., with a train originating at Montreal.

Photographer unknown
City Archives, Vancouver, B.C.

Plate 20

Massive early-day attempt to boost freight expeditiously over the heavy grades of the California Sierras was manifested by the grand experiment designed by A. J. Stevens and built at the Sacramento shops: locomotive No. 237 "El Gobernador" which, for a brief period, was among the most massive of American locomotives. A number of factors probably combined to make the attempt fruitless, not the least of which were the long rigid wheelbase implied by the five pairs of drivers and — doubtlessly the perennial bane of many heavy locomotives of the period — insufficient boiler steam generating capacity and overly large cylinders.

Photographer unknown
Everett L. DeGolyer, Jr. collection

Plate 21

In an attempt to instill sentiments of mutual interdependence and company loyalties, many railroads sponsored, or at least encouraged, group activities that in a college would be termed extracurricular. The Colorado Midland, for example, had a company band that during the brief existence of that line brought laurels far beyond those that might be ordinarily thought to characterize a soulless corporation.

On the Northern Pacific, America's National Game was it, judging by about 500 construction era pictures in the author's collection. Here is the Yakima & Pacific Coast Railroad baseball team of 1891.

Photographer unknown
DeGolyer Foundation Library

Plate 22

During the first several years of the presence of E. H. Harriman in the management of the Union Pacific railroad, the maintenance of way and bridges-and-buildings gangs were kept very busy indeed as they labored to convert an erstwhile operational disaster into one of the most modern and efficient of all American railroads. Wherever one travelled on the Union Pacific system, the impression was of magisterially directed turmoil. Iron and timber trusses were replaced by steel, bottlenecks were double tracked, and trestles were filled in.

Here is a splendid portrayal of Harriman-inspired activity at Papillion, Nebraska, about 1905.

J. E. Stimson photograph
Everett L. DeGolyer, Jr. collection

Plate 23

The James Bond of turn-of-the-century Union-Pacific officialdom was Superintendent of Motive Power William McKeen, Jr. McKeen was a true innovator in many fields of railroad equipment design. His best known artifacts are the "needle-nose" gasoline rail motor cars. The inspiration for the nautical motif characterizing these units is said to have occurred to McKeen as the result of a visit to the Herreshoff boat yard. The U.P. purchased many of these; eventually, McKeen was set up in business for himself in a corner of Omaha Shops, and sales were made to various other railroads.

McKeen also designed light-weight passenger cars and baggage cars to match his self-propelled units. One of the former is shown in this photo. Further innovations, which never seemed to find much acceptance, were light-weight box cars, and even a motor bus. You guessed it; the bus had porthole windows and round rear quarters.

The lady in white who usually adorned photos of McKeen equipment appears to be absent from this view made at 32nd Street suburban station, Omaha, Nebraska. She was *not* Phoebe Snow.

Union Pacific photograph
Everett L. DeGolyer, Jr. collection

Plate 24

Fortunately, a head-on collision is a rare event. This one, on the Oregon Railway & Navigation Co., a Union Pacific subsidiary took place east of The Dalles, Oregon, on trackage protected by automatic block signals. The photograph suggests that either one or both of the engine crews had overlooked their orders and that certainly both crews were ignoring signal indications. The Pacific type locomotives of both trains met with hideous force. The railway postoffice car of the regular train (to left) telescoped into the tender, as did the baggage car of Extra 3211 (to right). The fact that this latter car, although of steel construction, is nearly demolished would indicate that both trains were moving at high rates of speed.

Various clues indicate that this wreck occurred in the 1915-20 era.

Photographer unknown
DeGolyer Foundation Library

O. R. N. WRECK - EAST OF THE DALLES

Plate 25

As long as there are railroads, there will be work trains. The task of maintaining a constructed right of way is onerous; the constant rearrangement of existing trackage is an everyday necessity of life.

In 1956, Extra 428 exudes a patina of antiquity which could have characterized work train operation fifty years previous. The derrick is straight from the 1880s, and the pile driver behind is *echt* 1900 period Bucyrus-Erie. All cars of the usual rag-tag and bobtail diversity of castoffs which characterize equipment demoted to maintenance of way service. West of Ocento, Nebraska, and the last steam run of the year on the Stapleton line.

Francis Gschwind photograph

Plate 26

The most memorable modern passenger locomotives on the Union Pacific were the big Northern types of the FEF classes, of which the road owned 45 examples. These fine locomotives on test could develop 4,050 horsepower and could easily maintain speeds of 85 to 90 m.p.h. with fourteen car trains. When diesels took over most Union Pacific passenger runs, the Northerns were diverted to helper service and seasonal freight service. They performed nobly in these capacities right up to the end of the steam era, which came later on the Union Pacific than was the case with other western carriers. One of the Northerns, No. 844, now No. 8444 still runs on ceremonial occasions, the last functioning survivor of over a century of steam operation.

No. 829 smokes up the landscape east of North Platte, Nebraska, on an eastbound freight extra in September, 1958.

A. E. Stensvad photograph

Plate 27

People were still riding the cars in February, 1947, as is demonstrated by the 15-car consist of train No. 16, the eastbound Pacific Limited. The tonnage is obviously child's play for the big two-tone gray Northern type oil-burner on the head end, as it moves out of Shafer Siding, Idaho under a light haze of smoke.

H. R. Griffiths photograph

Plate 28

One of the Union Pacific's earlier oil turbine locomotives, as re-equipped with a fuel tender from a steam locomotive, is shown piloting Big Boy articulated No. 4015 out of Cheyenne yard on a westbound extra. The sonics of this pair must have been terrific — a howl with mushy chugging *continuo*. The turbines had a strident voice and a voracious appetite.

The Big Boys were also hungry — they burned 10 to 11 tons an hour of coal as they converted 50 to 55 tons of water into steam.

The combined horsepower of this muscular pair of units was 11,500!

Jim Ehernberger photograph

Plate 29

The ecclesiastically inspired station at Cheyenne was ordinarily busier than depicted in this photo. The eight tracks were often crowded as transcontinentals arrived in sections. However, on the twenty-first day of January, 1956, the sole occupant of these sprawling facilities is mixed train No. 52. The big Northern type No. 839 is more than sufficient unto its two-car task of this day. Ten days later will see the last run of this train.

Jim Ehernberger photograph

Plate 30

Green River, Wyoming, is famed for a number of reasons besides the innate hostility of the natives to peddlers of whatever sort. At the borders of towns throughout the Rocky Mountain west appears the admonition "Green River Ordinance Enforced", so it appears that the legal wisdom of the governing fathers of this town has generally been admired and, in fact, widely emulated.

Scenically speaking, the great sandstone-capped bluff, towering 300 feet above the town, has served as a backdrop for some of the most inspired portraits of the iron horse ever made.

The largest and most powerful of all Union Pacific locomotives is depicted upon the Green River turntable.

H. R. Griffiths photograph

Plate 31

Everything is Harriman Standard in this classic tableau of wintertime railroading at Wasatch, Utah. Obviously, the tank has sprung a series of leaks.

Richard Steinheimer photograph

Plate 32

Some of the landmark buildings of Salt Lake City, Utah, are shown in unusual juxtaposition to the Union Pacific yards as brought about by the employment of a powerful telephoto lens.

The city is one of the best laid-out in all North America, and its destinies have been linked with those of the Union Pacific railroad almost since its founding.

Richard Steinheimer photograph

Plate 33

As befits the status of the city as capital of Zion, the Union Pacific did its best for the civic self-esteem of Salt Lake City by the erection there of a monumental station. For reasons lost to posterity, the waiting room mural depicted only the Central Pacific end of the last spike ceremony at Promontory, Utah.

Richard Steinheimer photograph

Plate 34

One of the oddities of Cajon Pass, California, was the special signal installed at Summit, California to apprise oncoming traffic if a train were on its way up hill. Why ordinary colored light signals were not deemed sufficient remains unknown, but the contraption did work. It is shown lit up like a Christmas tree in honor of Union Pacific's ALCo-powered Extra 1621 in 1949.

Richard Steinheimer photograph

Plate 35

A very pleasant sound indeed was the gong of the dining car waiter who walked through the train and announced that mealtime was nigh.

The setting is aboard the Southern Pacific's "Daylight", bound for Los Angeles, just south of Palo Alto, California.

Richard Steinheimer photograph

Plate 36

"Dinner in the Diner — nothing could be finer"— and not
down south in Carolina, either. Very few railroads ever
achieved greater heights in peripatetic cuisine than the
Milwaukee Road; its "Dollar Dinner" on the nontrans-
continental "Pioneer Limited" of the 1920s is now a
legend to railroad gastronomists. The decor was truly in
keeping with that happy era when railroad travel was *the*
way to go. Short of the combined efforts of McCutcheon
and Plummers, it is scarcely possible to envisage a more
opulent display of linens, silver, and Chippewa Water
than that laid on for the patrons of the "Olympian",
sometime in the 1920s.

Company photograph
DeGolyer Foundation Library

Plate 37

An absolute "must" feature on western transcontinental trains was a barber shop. Journeys between Chicago and the Pacific coast were three-day, seventy-two-hour voyages and a man's thoughts were not apt to be interrupted by frequent phone calls en route. It was also a good time to freshen up one's personal appearance. Besides a barber, most limited trains of the period boasted a lady's maid and a valet. Other amenities of the trip were complimentary tea at 4:00 p.m. and the presence of a shower, or more rarely, a bathtub, in the lounge or observation cars.

Until the great speed-up of the 'forties, the trains were slow and comfortable. Along with the speed up to 39¾- and 48-hour trips, the amenities began to disappear.

Here is a splendid period-piece barber shop on the Milwaukee Road's "Olympian." The smooth operations obtaining on the road's stately electrified zones presumably did much to aid the straight-edge artist as he shaved the passengers.

Kaufman Weimer & Fabry photograph
DeGolyer Foundation Library

BARBER SHOP
"THE OLYMPIAN"

Plate 38

General Motors Corporation has always claimed that the original inspiration for the vista-dome car occurred to one of their vice presidents as he rode through Glenwood Canyon, Colorado, in the elevated cab of a "covered wagon".diesel freight locomotive. If you don't believe it, there is a monument across from Grizzly Creek siding to prove it.

The Burlington Route actually was the first to create a vista dome car in the modern era, by conversion of an already existing car which they renamed the "Silver Dome" in 1946. However, such units had existed in Canada on the Canadian Pacific Railway since 1906, and here is the interior of the first vista-dome observation car in North America. The architecture was obviously inspired by the time-honored caboose.

Canadian Pacific Railway photograph

7911

CANADIAN PACIFIC

7911

MPRS 3275. C.O. 2299. 4 OPEN OBSERVATION CARS. REBUILT. SERIES 7910-7913

Plate 40

The final dividend to a transcontinental journey on the Overland Route was the ferryboat trip between Oakland Mole and the Ferryboat Terminal at the foot of Market Street in San Francisco. The boat ride was one of the great scenic trips in the United States: Alcatraz, Treasure Island, the hills of San Francisco, and, in later years, the Bay and Golden Gate bridges. At one time, the S.P. had a huge fleet of ferryboats and, in addition to those boats needed for its own carrier functions, it had still others to cater to motorists.

The boats are all now a thing of the past, and it does not appear that it will be too many years hence until the trains will have joined them. Here is how it looked from the deck of the S.P. ferryboat *Berkeley* as it passed the company's "Sacramento" in 1950.

Richard Steinheimer photograph

Plate 41

Trademark of the Southern Pacific Lines in the steam era was its immense fleet of huge "cab-forward" locomotives. They constituted the lion's share of the road's group of "Articulated Consolidation" series, which was one of the largest fleets of articulated locomotives to be owned by any North American carrier.

The reason for this obverse operation is understandable when one considers the thirty-mile stretch of snow sheds the S.P. once had covering the original Central Pacific line over the crest of the Sierras. These structures could be best defined — in summer months — as tunnels with cracks, and in winter they were but tunnels. Their confined dimensions made them as near perfect gas chambers as any assembled by the Nazis in the 1930s, and there was no way to operate a large locomotive through them without asphyxiating its hapless engine-men. Empirical solution was to put the crew ahead of the exhaust by reversing the locomotive, not as complex an operation as it sounds, by virtue of the fact that they were all oil-fired.

No. 4141 is shown here at Crescent Lake on the "Shasta Line" in 1947. The crew is busy putting forward the best foot of the "Friendly" Southern Pacific.

Everett L. DeGolyer, Jr. photograph

Plate 42

The three classes of 5000-series Southern Pacific types were massive machines, albeit lacking the ferocious appearance of their counterparts on the Union Pacific, the ponderous and elongated three-cylinder Union Pacific types. The use of three cylinders, all simple expansion (one use of steam), looked like an excellent means of getting more power and better balance at relatively improved costs, but nasty maintenance problems arose involving the inaccessibility of both the crosshead of the center cylinder and the driver pair to which it was cranked. However, problems and all, the big 5000s served until the end of Southern Pacific steam operations as three-cylinder machines.

Paul Dailey photograph

Plate 43

Railroading is a stylized art with many features surviving in its conduct that have been present since its inception. Train movements are made by the book — that is, by employee's timetable, by the company book of rules, and by bulletin board and direct written orders from the train dispatcher.

Here, in one of the timeless rituals of railroading, a Southern Pacific conductor hands up the train orders to the engineer of a "Sunset Route" transcontinental train during a station stop.

Richard Steinheimer photograph

Plate 44

The air is filled with snow, and the American River completely invisible as the "City of San Francisco" rumbles upgrade, headed by three characteristic ALCo units. Around Cape Horn Curve, California.

Richard Steinheimer photograph

Plate 45

While the Tillamook branch of the Southern Pacific does not figure amongst its transcontinental preoccupations, no photographic representation of the company would be complete without a study by the late H. H. Arey of one of the freight trains on this line in the 1915 era. Arey, an S.P. engineer, was an accomplished cameraman, as this superior rendition of double-headed freight train No. 59, with two Mastodon types on the head end, at Cochran, Oregon, will show.

H. H. Arey photograph
DeGolyer Foundation Library

Plate 46

Taylor hump yards at Los Angeles, California, are among the most important on the Southern Pacific. Like most features of main line railroading, they are a twenty-four-hours-per-day operation.

Here a series of cars is weighed and classified as it goes over the hump.

Plate 47

The name of this sylvan location is Big Timber, Montana, and Mikado type No. 1908 hustles a westbound freight along the line in one of the perceptive capturings of the mood of wintertime railroading in the west, 1953.

Richard Steinheimer photograph

Plate 48

Westernmost outpost of the 15,000 Southern Pacific system at its height in 1946 was Oakland Mole at Oakland, California. Here was the westernmost reach of the original Overland Route, and the southernmost portion of the Siskiyou and Shasta Lines from Oregon. From here, San Francisco could be reached by one of the most magical of all ferryboat rides in North America, a perfect complement to any transcontinental journey.

Unfortunately, the customers went elsewhere after World War II. Who is there to deny the speedy potentialities of the Boeing 707? Who indeed is to disclaim the apparently more economic charms of the family automobile, with unlimited stopovers, to boot?

In any event, the patronage went elsewhere. The Southern Pacific Company eventually did away with the boats, and then cut back the trains to downtown Oakland. Motorbuses then made the connection to downtown San Francisco.

It is, at this point, highly doubtful if anything can be done to win the patronage back to the cars. It seems unlikely that anyone who is propelled by necessity to make a transcontinental journey is going to spend a minimum of 55 hours to accomplish what can be performed more economically, all costs included, in six. Safety considerations are of little moment; a train is one of the safest of all conveyances, an airplane perhaps one of the more hazardous, but neither can rival in hazard the joys of the automobile that one will undoubtedly rent at the conclusion of the trip. The American public has always entertained a penchant for hazard in regard to its choice of public transportation.

Here is an illustration of the times when expectations of speed were not as high and when scenic expectations were greater. Subsidiary Northwestern Pacific's ten-wheeler No. 183 has just brought in a passenger extra upon the Oakland Mole; steam ferryboat *Berkeley* is ready to convey all passengers across the scenic reaches of San Francisco Bay.

Richard Steinheimer photograph

Plate 49

Bell-cow passenger train of the Northern Pacific Railroad is the beautiful vista dome "North Coast Limited", train No. 25, Chicago to Seattle, and, via the connecting Spokane, Portland & Seattle Railway, to Portland. Not quite as spectacularly equipped as the "California Zephyr", the train has been creating a favorable patronage since its first run on April 29, 1900.

The observation car is now gone, a reminder of the grim economics of the operation of transcontinental trains, and the lounge for Pullman passengers has migrated to the vista dome of the sleeping car, but the train is a handsome sight this day in 1964 as she flashes through Willow Creek, Montana, paralleling the electrified trackage of the Milwaukee Road.

Richard Steinheimer photograph

Plate 50

It is a thoroughly nasty day as a cold wind whips wet snow through the air at Jamestown, North Dakota. The time has come for the Northern Pacific's "North Coast Limited" to depart on another lap of the lengthy journey between Chicago and the Pacific Coast. The conductor waves a highball.

Richard Steinheimer photograph

Plate 51

The Northern Pacific had for many years a running battle with the railroad commissioners of North Dakota. The regulators were great believers in the virtues of branch-line passenger trains, and the railroad was forced to run them, regardless of whether or not anyone wanted to ride on them. Out of Jamestown, N.D., for example, branch-line trains ran to Wilton, Oakes, and Leeds, and continued to do so until very late in the game indeed.

In order to cut expenses, the company relied on its aging fleet of gas-electric cars and the roundhouse at Jamestown was full of them. The chief advantage, besides their economical consumption of fuel, was that they could be operated with a three-man crew: engineer, conductor and baggageman.

At night, these cars were idle and their characteristic brightly painted noses added their part to the interplay of bright light and shadow that is a roundhouse in the wee hours. An essential, but unpaid, member of the company's forces makes her rounds.

Richard Steinheimer photograph

Plate 52

This ghastly apparition in the Northern Pacific round-house at Jamestown, N.D., is a very unusual bit of equipment indeed. It is, in fact, a rotary snow plow, but apparently a model equipped wtih a complete extra set of whirring dentures. Its proud, but unknown, manufacturers probably catalogued the model as "The Great Masticator".

Richard Steinheimer photograph

Plate 53

It is very late in the evening indeed as old Northern Pacific model FT diesels prepare to move a southbound freight train bound for Portland, Oregon, out of the yards at Tacoma, Washington.

The model FT (as in Freight) diesels were the locomotives that brought a quick and sudden end to the use of steam locomotives in North America. The Buick Roadmaster style of body design (complete with portholes) now looks dated, but these were among the pioneer diesel road freight locomotives of them all. May, 1964.

Richard Steinheimer photograph

Plate 54

This grim-visaged trio of gentlemen is of mien entirely appropriate to the seriousness of this day's occasions. They are, left to right, Mark V. Potter, Harry E. Byram, and E. W. Brundage. They are, by profession, the receivers of the Chicago, Milwaukee and St. Paul Railway. The day is November 22, 1926 and the location is Butte, Montana. The receivers are here to hold an auction of the company's properties to satisfy fore-closure by holders of the railroad's mortgage bonds. There will not be many bidders as the minimum bid is rather stiff, $122,500,000.

Actually, the sale was quite successful. There was but one bid, that of the new company, which was a rousing figure, $140,000.000.

Unfortunately, the new company was not much more successful than the old, and within seven and a half years, the board of directors was again pounding the doors of the Federal Court House at Chicago and seeking the protection of his honor.

Photographer unknown
Arthur D. Dubin collection

Plate 55

Only a sublime confidence in the massive construction of the front drawbars and draft-gears of the respective equipment involved could have countenanced this push-of-war contest between bipolar electric No. 10254 and mallet No. 9520, held on the Cascade Division on February 22, 1920. It was really a bit unfair, as the electric had 24 low drivers versus the 12 higher ones of the large steam locomotive. At this precise second, No. 10254 has won hands down. Reaching skyward for every possible kilowatt hour with both of her great pantographs, she is slowly easing back the protesting steam power, which we may be certain has the Johnson bar in the corner. Come to think of it, probably the most implausible action photo ever made.

General Electric Co. photograph
DeGolyer Foundation Library

Plate 56

The mountain-leveling characteristics of the famous bipolar electrics are attractively illustrated in this Asahel Curtis rendition of No. 10251 in her youth. While nothing before — or since — put on rails ever had a more startling profile, the electrical technology involved went straight back to the pioneer N.Y.C. & H.R.R.R. electrics of 1906, which brought smokeless power into the heart of Manhattan at Grand Central Station.

Baseball immortal Babe Ruth holds the fireman's seat here.

Asahel Curtis photograph
Donald Duke collection

10251

UTAH

50576
ASAHEL CURTIS

Plate 57

Having spent unaccountably extravagant sums on its Puget Sound extension and then even further millions on the heroic electrified zones of the road, the Milwaukee Road was not about to have the ozone-laden precincts of its yards polluted by the exhausts of coal burning steam locomotives.

The result was the purchase of a number of electric switch engines. These were basically standard interurban-type freight locomotives with pantographs instead of trolley poles.

One of the last of these is switching at Butte, Montana, in 1956.

Richard Steinheimer photograph

Plate 58

It is difficult if not impossible today to recollect what beehives of human activity were once represented by division-point roundhouses. Until the late 1930s, multiple division runs were comparatively unknown; every 125 miles, more or less, locomotives were exchanged for replacement as were fresh mounts on the Pony Express.

Miles City, Montana, is the apogee of locomotive changes, grate shakedowns, and boiler washes that characterized transcontinental railroading as it was practiced in the steam era of the Great Depression.

Photographer unknown
S. R. Wood collection

Plate 59

Among the oldest locomotives in use today on any major railroad are the few surviving General Electric locomotives employed in helper service on the Milwaukee Railroad. They were formerly employed in freight and passenger service on the electrified system operated by that carrier.

Electric motive power is seemingly indestructible. It has been a good many years ago that the company auditors celebrated the fiftieth birthday of E-25, but the four units comprising this big locomotive, doubtlessly kept in operating condition by parts cannibalized from defunct sister units, are ready to add their considerable power to assist the diesels in boosting tonnage up the flanks of Snoqualmie Pass.

The night is both cold and rainy, and the end for the electrified zone is probably not far away.

Richard Steinheimer photograph

Plate 60

Engineer Adam Gratz smiles bemusedly as he successfully urges his fifty-year-old electric locomotive into regenerative braking "the old way" down the east flanks of Snoqualmie Pass, Washington.

Regenerative braking was first employed on electrics. The principle is that downhill, the motors act as generators and actually send back to the overhead wires a good deal of the energy that was required to lift them uphill. The action slows the train down appreciably, and saves a great deal of wear and tear on brakes and wheels.

Diesels, too, have regenerative braking, but the electricity created is sent to large grids, whereat it is dissipated as heat.

M. M. Snelson photograph

Plate 61

Originally two-unit locomotives, the big General Electrics were rebuilt to three or four units in freight configuration with cabs and pony trucks removed on intermediate units. At least one photo exists to portray one unit as the Deer Lodge Switcher. Both halves were separately operable.

Today, No. E-38 is in freight service as it purrs quietly through the icy beauty of the Montana Rockies.

Richard Steinheimer photograph

Plate 62

While Westinghouse managed to share some portion of the fiscal solace attendant upon being a purveyor of electric locomotive power to the nation's longest (in route miles) electrified system, it did not seem, retrospectively, to have been as quick to dispatch its company photographers to the untrammeled wilds of the Bitter Roots and Cascades as was General Electric. Nevertheless, graphic efforts were made, as is attested by this view of No. 10307 at the head end of the "Olympian", made by the tireless Asahel Curtis on the Pacific side of the Bitter Roots. The burned areas date from the great forest fire of 1910.

Asahel Curtis photograph
Donald Duke collection

Plate 63

The "Olympian Hiawatha" has just disgorged the last sack of mail and the last frayed trunk as it prepares to depart from Butte, Montana.

Richard Steinheimer photograph

Plate 64

Railroads have long served the cattle and ranching industry. Here cowboys of the Sappington Hereford Ranch are busy in the stock pens at Willow Creek, Montana, as a couple of the Milwaukee Road's "Little Joes" add a few cars of eastbound livestock to the time freight.

Recent changes in the geographical and economic conditions of the meat-packing industry have seen a great decline in the shipment of livestock by rail.

Richard Steinheimer photograph

Plate 65

A railroad possessing such highly individualistic power as the Milwaukee could scarcely be expected to ease into the dieselized era with the same locomotives as those possessed by any of its competitors. It went to home-state engine manufacturer Fairbanks-Morse who, in turn, joined forces with the Locomotive and Spare Parts Department of the General Electric Company at Erie, Pennsylvania, and the result was the Barbra Streisand nose of No. 5. Invisible within the shining profile of this locomotive were thirty cylinders chortling away in merry opposition to each other and six traction motors, all combining to produce 6,000 horsepower.

Company photograph
DeGolyer Foundation Library

MAR 26 - 1947

Plate 66

Railroading is a twenty-four-hour-a-day operation and the trains never cease to rumble through town the year around. It is about 1:00 a.m. at Plummer Junction, Washington, as the operator makes up a batch of train orders to be hooped up to the conductor and engineer of a passing freight.

Richard Steinheimer photograph

Plate 67

The most absolute type of stop signal employed in railroading is the smash-board. If not obeyed and run, all of the signal arm and part of the front end of the locomotive are going to be missing, with a resultant journey of the errant engineer to the carpet of management, a voyage painful to contemplate.

Here is one on the Milwaukee's main line at Deer Lodge, Montana, set at its most positive prohibitory admonition, as the N.P. local bound to Garrison, Montana, creeps across the main.

Richard Steinheimer photograph

Plate 68

Most magnificent of all Santa Fe Railway steam passenger locomotives were the huge Northern types of the 2900 and 3780 classes. Both were the largest, fastest, most powerful and most efficient of this type ever to have been built. They were also among the last steam locomotives to operate on the Santa Fe system.

This night picture at San Diego, California, shows what was to be among the final chores of the big Northerns — assignment to extra sections of the "San Diegan" trains. About 1952.

Richard Steinheimer photograph

Plate 69

In the center, the high level "El Capitan" has just pulled into the station at Albuquerque, New Mexico. It has just disgorged a hoard of passengers, many of whom are making a bee-line for the Fred Harvey store specializing in Indian artifacts.

To the right is the "El Pasoan", the Albuquerque-to-El Paso, Texas, train. Before the Santa Fe got all the way to Los Angeles on its own tracks, it used to form a through route to California by interchange with the Southern Pacific at El Paso.

The "El Pasoan" is now another among the large number of vanished passenger trains.

Richard Steinheimer photograph

Plate 70

Counterpart of the "Super Chief" is the all-coach high-level "El Capitan". Most of the year, it is run as a consolidated train with the "Super Chief", but at periods of peak traffic, it enjoys an autonomous schedule and its own drumhead.

Architecturally, the "El Capitan" is one of the most interesting trains in the world. Its cars are the same 85-foot length as any other modern-era passenger equipment, but much higher. They are literally two-story cars. Each has the capacity of two conventional cars, though the space allotted to each passenger is just the same as on the older equipment. However, toilets and washrooms are on the ground floor. They are probably the most comfortable passenger cars ever built.

Communication throughout the train is at the level of the upper story. Certain cars are high level at one vestibule and low level at the other so that they may be run in the same train with conventional equipment.

It is summer, and the "El Capitan" is a separate train, composed entirely of high-level equipment. It is departing the Raton, New Mexico, station.

Everett L. DeGolyer, Jr. photograph

Plate 71

The little town of Raton, New Mexico, has been a center of helper locomotive activity ever since the Santa Fe Railway built over Raton Pass. While the switchbacks with their six per cent grades were abolished in the construction era, the main line still has maximum grades of three per cent, which call for the frequent addition of power to eastbound trains at Raton. Conversely, it is occasionally necessary to add helpers to westbound trains at Trinidad, Colorado, on the other side of the pass.

Most Santa Fe freight service from Chicago to the west coast moves via the Belen cut-off with its low grades. Consequently, the locomotive turning facilities at Raton have become increasingly less used.

Here three big ALCo road switchers idle away during the night. The exhaust of their big diesels is characteristically jagged; each revolution of the crankshaft suggests that it may be the last.

Richard Steinheimer photograph

Plate 72

Premier eastbound and San Francisco-originating train of the Santa Fe Railway is the "San Francisco Chief". It is shown departing from Gallup, New Mexico, with its four big ALCo diesels sending up a plume of smoke that would have delighted the late Lucius Beebe.

The "San Francisco Chief" has a veritable smorgasbord of equipment with both high- and low-level coaches and a full-length dome car that provide the last remaining passenger service from San Francisco to Chicago via the Belen cut-off.

Richard Steinheimer photograph

Plate 73

On a day well below zero in December, 1950, a massive Rio Grande-Santa Fe type gets a move on a long string of empty coal cars somewhere near Helper, Utah. Helper is one of those appropriately named railroad towns, where helper locomotives are added on to assist trains over the heavy grades leading to Soldier Summit.

Richard Steinheimer photograph

Plate 74

When a passenger detrains from the Santa Fe Railway's "San Francisco Chief", he has just left one of the most luxuriously equipped passenger trains running in the United States. If he steps into the waiting room at Mountainair, New Mexico, he will have collided head on with the nineteenth century as is mutely attested by this photograph.

Richard Steinheimer photograph

Plate 75

Winter has come to Williams Junction, Arizona, as a long Santa Fe diesel-powered freight train pulls by.

The location is a latter-day addition to the railroad's timetable and is the point of departure for the railroad's line south to Phoenix. Until recently, it was also the point where Pullman cars were set out for the branch-line run up to Grand Canyon, but this is another amenity of railroad travel which has disappeared.

Richard Steinheimer photograph

Plate 76

Doubleheading was an infrequent event upon the Texas & Pacific Railway, whose taste in matters of locomotive design tended towards large, imposing and powerful machines which could handle alone anything that was likely to be attached to their rear tender drawbar. On rare occasions, however, it did happen, and the results were often photographically imposing.

Here one-of-a-kind Pacific No. 700 adds her not-inconsiderable tractive effort of Mountain-type No. 906 on the eastbound "Southerner", train No. 8, bound from El Paso to St. Louis and New Orleans, in 1940, out of Dallas Union Terminal.

Charles Van Winkle photograph

Plate 77

The station at Terrell, Texas, was a fanciful job in brick and once served both the Texas & Pacific and the Texas Midland railroads. The latter company was for years the corporate child of playboy Colonel E.H.R. Green. At one time, it served at least fourteen daily passenger trains bound to the four cardinal points of the compass.

There's not much passenger activity at Terrell anymore. The T&P is down to one daily train in each direction, petition for the abandonment of which has been filed. The Texas Midland, taken over by the Southern Pacific in the mid 1920s, has largely been abandoned.

Dean Hale photograph

Plate 78

A sight to thoroughly confuse any passing locomotive engineer was the big gantry at the western end of the Dallas Union Terminal Company's junction with the Texas & Pacific main line. The tower had temporarily been dismantled for maintenance and in order to avoid confusion, all signals were oriented at a 90-degree angle to the track. Upon reassembly, everything was restored to rights.

Everett L. DeGolyer, Jr. photograph

Plate 79

The Texas & Pacific Railway's "Texas Eagle" train, west-bound, rattles briskly over the Missouri-Kansas-Texas R.R. crossing at Cisco, Texas. The "Eagle" is bound for El Paso and includes in its economy a Pullman car originating in Dallas which will be delivered to the Southern Pacific at El Paso for delivery via the "Sunset Limited" to Los Angeles.

The "Eagle" has long since been discontinued west of Fort Worth; the Texas & Pacific has lost its once separate identity from parent Missouri Pacific; and most of the *Katy's* former Texas Central line has been demolished.

Everett L. DeGolyer, Jr. photograph

Plate 80

The "Empire Builder", named for founding father James J. Hill, is the finest effort of the Great Northern Railway. While in common with most other western passenger trains it seems to have, at best, a limited future life, it is still one of the most handsome trains in the union, exceeded in lavishness of dome equipment only by the "California Zephyr".

Its resplendent scheme of olive drab, yellow, and orange has since been repainted a solid "Glacier Park blue", but its daily trip from Chicago (via Burlington) to St. Paul, thence to Seattle and to Portland (via Spokane, Portland & Seattle Railway) is still one of the outstanding treats in railroad passenger travel.

Here, the "Empire Builder" approaches the snowsheds near Browning, Montana, which have been demolished since this view was made in May 1964.

Richard Steinheimer photograph

Plate 81

An infrequently photographed event was the transcontinental dash of a silk express train. The late 1920s were the high point of the use of this fabric for dressmaking purposes and raw silk, landed from Japan at Seattle, Washington, was rushed across the continent at the highest possible speeds for deliveries to the mills at Paterson, New Jersey.

The Great Northern Railway was a prime avenue of this high-tariff and high-insurance-premium traffic and got the trains over its main line with a maximum of expedition. Here a silk train pauses briefly en route at New Rockford, North Dakota, in September 1925, behind locomotive No. 2517, one of the road's big Baldwin Mountain types.

While this is a time exposure, it is an attractive rendition as the blurred forms of the members of the engine crew convey something of the frantic purposefulness with which these runs were attended.

Great Northern Railway photograph

Plate 82

The scene here is Skynomish, Washington, the western locomotive change point for the eight-mile trip through the Cascade Tunnel, the longest in North America. Actually, the electrics formerly operated to Appleyard, 72.86 miles beyond Skynomish, and in the pre-diesel days, provided a clean trip through the lengthy depths of the long tunnel.

This electric line is no more, the diesel having eliminated any difficulties of ventilation that would have been encountered in the steam era. The "Western Star" is making a station stop, and then will continue, alone and unaided, through the Cascade Tunnel.

Richard Steinheimer photograph

Plate 83

All is calm and peaceful in the Montana Rockies surrounding the Essex station and even though the date is as late as May, 1964, there is still much snow on the ground. Down at the city dump, the grizzly bears prowl the garbage unmolested.

Richard Steinheimer photograph

Plate 84

The long standing motto of the Denver & Rio Grande Western Railroad "Through the Rockies and Not Around Them" is epitomized by this photograph made by an unknown photographer in the mid nineteen-thirties. Here the handsome and graceful Northern-type locomotive No. 1700 sweeps into Hanging Bridge Station with the westbound "Scenic Limited", where it will pause ten minutes for its complement of passengers to detrain and marvel at this most railroad-oriented of western wonders.

Plate 85

The frontal assault upon the Rocky Mountains made by the late David H. Moffatt is one of the most astounding stretches of line to be found in the United States. Only the eastern approach to Hagerman Pass of the Colorado Midland Railroad would come close to approaching it as an utter example of virtuosity in sinuosity.

The eastbound SFO symbol freight is shown coasting downhill with dynamic brakes whining, headed by four modern-day high horsepower diesel road switchers.

Richard Steinheimer photograph

Plate 86

The Rio Grande was in a spasm of construction activities in the early 1880s. As well as hurling its rails westward to Leadville, it made an unsuccessful lunge towards Raton Pass. If all of this activity were not enough to sap the expansionistic energies of General William Jackson Palmer, further forays were made towards the far-off San Juan. The Rio Grande had been completed from Pueblo to La Veta in 1876. In 1878, it progressed to Alamosa, and by 1881, its tracks were in Durango. Finally, in 1882, it had arrived at the mining camp of Silverton, deep within the San Juan Range.

In order to cover the southernmost portion of the State of Colorado, the Rio Grande once again was forced to scale the Continental Divide. This it did at Cumbres, Colorado, at an elevation of 10,015 feet. The eastern approach was easy enough, with maximum grades of only 1.42 percent, but the western entrance was again one of those nasty operating problems in which the baby railroad seemed to abound, a steady 4 feet per 100-foot rise from the little New Mexico town of Chama to Cumbres Pass.

One of the nation's most notably lamented passenger trains, the narrow gauge "San Juan", pauses at Cumbres, Colorado, on January 25, 1951. The end of her journeys will occur within days. The covered Wye at the summit is to the right.

Joseph Schick photograph

Plate 87

In the steam era of railroading, the most typical of all railroad structures were water tanks. This one, at Del Norte, Colorado, is equipped to serve two thirsty locomotives simultaneously, though it is doubtful if this often happened as traffic was sparse on the Creede branch.

Consolidation No. 1167 was one of the last standard gauge steam locomotives to be running on the Rio Grande railroad.

James Ehernberger photograph

Plate 88

An infrequently photographed sight is a brand-new locomotive en route from the manufacturer to its new owner. The general custom was to send them out dead in slow freight trains with main-rods removed. Each locomotive was accompanied by an engine-messenger, an employee of the locomotive works, who pitched a rather comfortless camp in the cab for the matter of the several days it took to get them west. His principal job was to see that all journals were running cool and kept well lubricated. He snatched whatever sleep he could between stops, and doubtless ate whenever he was able. The task was cold in winter, hot in summer and offered minimal on-the-job comforts at all times. At the best, it was a good slow-speed way to see the country.

Here is Rio Grande R.R. No. 3711 en route from Eddystone, Pennsylvania, to Pueblo, Colorado, at East St. Louis, Illinois, in 1942.

Photographer unknown
Everett L. DeGolyer, Jr. collection

Plate 89

The Moffat Tunnel having been transversed, the ''California Zephyr'' heads towards the headwaters of the Colorado River, which it encounters near Kremmling. It will follow these through Gore Canon, in which it runs down to Dotsero. At this point, the train turns west, and shortly enters Glenwood Canon, having in the meantime crossed from the north to the south bank of the river.

The eastbound ''California Zephyr'' passes Grizzly siding, named for Grizzly Creek, a local topographical feature. At this point, there is a monument to the vista-dome car, the inspiration for which occurred to a General Motors executive as he gazed upwards at the massive sides of Glenwood Canon from his elevated perch in the cab of a diesel locomotive.

Everett L. DeGolyer, Jr. photograph

Plate 90

Some of the most grandiose of all western scenery is to be found at the highest point on the Overland Route of the Southern Pacific high up in the Sierra Mountains of California. Below the tracks and far down the mountain-side lies Donner Lake. Both are named for the tragic emigrant party which met its fate near this spot over 100 years previously.

Something of the forbidding and hostile character of this snow-covered area is conveyed in this magnificent winter photo by Richard Steinheimer. An unusual sight is the eastbound "California Zephyr" of the Western Pacific, today making a detour over the tracks of its competition.

Richard Steinheimer photograph

Plate 91

The old tunnel at Tennessee Pass, Colorado, was 2,577 feet long and its western portal was at an altitude of 10,239 feet.

During World War II, transcontinental traffic boomed over the Royal Gorge Line. The dimensions of the tunnel were none too liberal to begin with, and the infirmities of old age became too onerous a hindrance to the daily operation of the railroad to be tolerated. Consequently, in the years 1944-1945, a new tunnel was holed through. The new tunnel wasn't much shorter, 2,500 feet, and did not lower the summit to any great extent, crossing the Continental Divide at 10,221 feet. However, its concrete-lined interior made for greatly decreased maintenance, and height was sufficiently liberal for the new generation of high-rise rolling stock built after World War II.

Here are the old and new tunnels at Tennessee Pass with a westbound freight topping the Continental Divide.

Richard Steinheimer photograph

Plate 92

The Denver & Rio Grande handily beat the Colorado Midland into the great mining town of Aspen, Colorado. The first Rio Grande passenger trains arrived at Aspen on the evening of November 1, 1887. By virtue of their earlier arrival upon the scene, they held the north side of the Roaring Fork River, topographically a much easier site upon which to build a railroad. The Midland built along the south side of the Roaring Fork. (Today, Colorado State Highway 82 occupies the former C.M. right-of-way from east of Basalt almost into Aspen.) This necessitated the construction of a tremendous iron viaduct across Maroon Creek, just to the west of town, and the complications attending the erection of this structure detained the entry of the Midland into Aspen until February 4, 1888.

The arrival of the Rio Grande sent the citizenry of Aspen into a tremendous whing-ding celebration. No doubt, some of them still had flannel-coated tongues dating back to this party, because the arrival of the Midland three months later occasioned no such jubilation. Aspenites had little enough to celebrate for a long time to come, as the repeal of the Silver Purchase Act in 1893 caused a twilight to come about on the fortunes of this town that was to continue for over fifty years.

During these five decades, the population of Aspen diminished from over 10,000 inhabitants to as few as 500 to 700 people by 1936. Oddly enough, some of the original business of the town managed to survive despite a depression that had continued for so long a time.
The little newspaper *The Aspen Times* went from a daily to a weekly, but continued regular publication as it had since 1881. Beck and Bishop, grocers, continued to feed the hungry.

In 1945-1946, a renaissance came to the affairs of Aspen that is still very much under way. Gradually, the town became a cultural and ski resort. Pitkin County (of which Aspen is the seat) managed to field over 2,500 voters in the 1968 presidential election. A town of miners and stockmen became a small city of inn-keepers. (The town can now sleep over 7,000 transients a night!)

The Midland abandoned service to Aspen in 1918, and the Rio Grande undoubtedly considered doing so in the vexatious years that followed. In the mid 1950s, a boom occurred in mining, this time in iron ore rather than silver, and traffic on the Aspen branch improved to the extent that the Rio Grande ran a twenty-car freight of iron ore each weekday out of Woody Creek siding.

We see the five-days-a-week ore train burbling down the steady two-percent descending grade near Bates siding.

Everett L. DeGolyer, Jr. photograph

Plate 93

Emma, Colorado, was once quite a busy point on the Aspen branch of the Rio Grande. It had a station, which also served nearby Basalt, a water tank, stock-pens, several sidings and a one-room school house. After about 1900, the town had a general store, substantially built of brick, with a large brick feed-storage bin behind.

This part of the Roaring Fork Valley was (and is) quite a center of ranching. The railroad originated a good many carloads of sheep and cattle here, and terminated, at certain times of the year, a number of carloads of grapes. These were made into wine by the local citizenry. (It might be noted that many of the oldest families in this part of the valley are of Italian ancestry.) Other traffic was in potatoes, no longer raised hereabouts, but once acclaimed as a fine seed stock.

Time has passed Emma by. The general store has been closed for many years, as is the school. The station and water tank were demolished at least a decade ago. The livestock moves by truck and it would appear that homemade wine is one of the lost arts. The last signs of Emma as a focal point of railroading were the stock pens and this picturesque string of disused maintenance-of-way cars. Today, these are also gone, and only the main track to Aspen is there to mark the time when this hamlet was a point of some importance to the railroad.

Everett L. DeGolyer, Jr. photograph

Plate 94

The decline of the passenger train has been attended by the decline of the rural town. The extent to which these respective declines are correlated is unknown to this writer, but both do exist.

An accompanying result has been the vanishing type of indigenous American architecture represented by the rural station. What few still exist are mandatory for operating purposes. Here is one of the very few left on the eastern end of the Royal Gorge line of the Rio Grande, at Texas Creek, Colorado, with all regulation paraphernalia in view.

At one time, Texas Creek was junction point for the hairy branch line to Westcliffe, abandoned since 1938.

Everett L. DeGolyer, Jr. photograph

Plate 95

While the "California Zephyr" was one of the comparatively few success stories of post World War II railroading, the Western Pacific had another pair of passenger trains, numbers 1 and 2, once y-clept "The Royal Gorge", that produced scant passenger satisfaction and much red ink as they wearily plodded their way across the deserts of Nevada and Utah.

Despite a hearty and oft-expressed desire to banish these runs from its timetable forever, the W.P. had repeated cornfield meets with the California Railroad Commission, a body singular in its implacable opposition to passenger train discontinuances, regardless of whether or not the number of train employees exceeded the number of passengers.

To make the best of an unfavorable regulatory climate, the W.P. purchased in 1952 a pair of RDC cars, which offered numerous benefits in cost savings over locomotive hauled trains, not only in fuel and maintenance, but also reduced crew requirements. These offered a tri-weekly service to the lonesome little towns along the main line which were not even conditional stops for the lordly "California Zephyrs". Numbers 1 and 2 once again had a name, they were now "Zephyrettes".

By 1960, even the infrequent Basque shepherd or prospector had gone elsewhere to satisfy his occasional transportation needs, and trains 1 and 2 passed on into history.

It is about 6:30 p.m. and the engineer and fireman give No. 172 a final check as she prepares to embark upon the long trip from Oakland mole to Salt Lake City.

Richard Steinheimer photograph

Plate 96

It is before dawn at Salt Lake City, and the Western Pacific (locomotive at left) has just delivered the "California Zephyr" to the Rio Grande for 570 consecutive mountain-bordered miles of the Wasatches and Rockies, a dawn-to-dusk journey.

Richard Steinheimer photograph

Plate 97

One of the last two remaining examples of Colorado Midland Railway rolling stock is observation chair car No. 111, which today reposes in the Colorado Railroad Museum at Golden.

A record of its peregrinations would include almost every major gold and silver camp served by rail in the Centennial State except Creede. It was fittingly included in the consist of the last passenger movement ever run over the former rails of the Colorado Midland, between Colorado Springs and Divide on the Midland Terminal Railway in 1949.

Everett L. DeGolyer, Jr. photograph

Plate 98

One of the most picturesque sets of ruins to be found on the former lines of the Colorado Midland Railway was the battery of charcoal ovens at Seller, Colorado, high up on the western approaches to the Busk-Ivanhoe tunnel. The wooden hoops strengthening the brickwork on these old ovens have long since warped and weathered into a fantastic variety of shapes.

Seller was once an exceptionally important adjunct to Colorado Midland operations and a visit to this railroad ghost town is still of consuming interest.

The ovens supplied charcoal as fuel to the smelters at Leadville for a number of years after the completion of the Colorado Midland.

Everett L. DeGolyer, Jr. photograph

Plate 99

One of the least-well-known sights in the resort town of Aspen, Colorado, is the underpinnings of the great iron bridge at Maroon Creek. The bridge served the railroad faithfully from its installation in late 1887. Following the abandonment of the Colorado Midland in 1921, it has carried the traffic of Colorado State Highway 82, with only a moderate amount of subsequent reinforcement.

The bridge deserves to be better known as one of the finest examples of nineteenth century bridge engineering, as well as the biggest remaining artifact of a romantic and improbable mountain railroad.

Everett L. DeGolyer, Jr. photograph

Plate 100

The author would like to pause here a moment to deliver a brief sermon on the chowder-headed idiocy of many of his brother railroad buffs, particularly those who take pictures. A large and vocal segment of them, particularly those who have been in the game a long time, cannot see beyond the locomotive and, unless it is a steam locomotive, cannot even see that. This group is to be pitied; they are now obviously under-employed. There are sub-groups even in such a major group as this; one, for example, would not make pictures of locomotives that were stored; another group would make nothing but smokey action shots; still another would not make pictures of locomotives after 9:00 a.m. nor before 4:00 p.m. and then only with the side rods down. Many of the younger generation of enthusiasts are bored by steam locomotives — and why not? They are children of the internal combustion age.

In the meantime, the heavy-weight passenger car has disappeared. First-generation diesels are worth a whoop and a holler on the rare occasions one can unearth them. The rural station has disappeared. The passenger train is disappearing. If there is a structures specialist, no one has yet found him.

In 1959, the author went to make a sentimental pilgrimage to the old Midland Terminal Railway. He had chased the five-and six-locomotive-powered trains of empty gondolas up Ute Pass, camera in hand, as a teenager. Now the railroad had been gone and for the most part few artifacts were left to mark its passing other than the mute snow-covered ridges that were once its right-of-way. There was a boarded-up station here, some old car bodies there. Yet the most interesting find of all was the fire station and town hall of Goldfield, Colorado. The author likes to think that it tells something about the railroad, its place and its era, even if it does not possess a headlight, smokestack, bell or whistle.

Everett L. DeGolyer, Jr. photograph

Plate 101

The middle 1960s have been a most unhappy time for those who love passenger trains. Wholesale discontinuance of passenger trains has been the order of the day. Not only large cities, but whole states are now denoted as "freight service only" in the *Official Guide.*

One alternative to complete discontinuance is the consolidation of trains in off-peak periods, and few managements have been more skillful at this latter-day accomplishment than that of the Union Pacific, as is mutely attested by the train bulletin board at Riverside, California.

Richard Steinheimer photograph

TIME TABLE

NOV 18

WEST BOUND				EAST BOUND		
Nº	TRAIN	DUE	REMARKS	Nº	TRAIN	DUE	REMARKS
5	PASSENGER	4:30 A.M.		116	LAS VEGAS HOLIDAY SPECIAL	8:20 A.M.	920
103	CITY OF LOS ANGELES	12:10 P.M.		104	CITY OF ST. LOUIS	1:55 P.M.	
103	CHALLENGER	12:10 P.M.	ON TIME	104	CHALLENGER	1:55 P.M.	ONE TRAIN
103	CITY OF ST. LOUIS	12:10 P.M.		104	CITY OF LOS ANGELES	1:55 P.M.	
115	LAS VEGAS HOLIDAY SPECIAL	9:55 P.M.		6	PASSENGER	10:35 P.M.	

Plate 102

It positively pained the author of this book to have to go out and make this picture, but the truth must be told, even when it hurts.

This picture might be entitled "Christmas Rush at Dallas, Texas, Union Terminal". Gone is the Santa Fe to Chicago, Houston and to California. Gone is the Southern Pacific to Denison, Beaumont, Houston and California. Gone is the Frisco to Tulsa and to Fort Worth. Gone is the Katy to St. Louis, San Antonio and Denton. Gone is the Cotton Belt to Memphis and to St. Louis. Gone is the Rock Island to Minneapolis and to Houston. Gone is the Burlington Route to Denver and to Houston. Gone is the United States Mail.

The car cleaners are furloughed. The upholsterers are furloughed. The car men are furloughed. The switching crew is furloughed. The Pullman Company office has long since been shut down. The locomotive has been sold.

The time — December 14, 1968 — Happy New Year!

Everett L. DeGolyer, Jr. photograph

Plate 103

By the Centennial of Promontory, the American nation is on the move.

Of all forms of intercity travel, the automobile is by far the most prevalently used. It accounts for 92 percent of journeys made. The airlines, buslines and railroads compete for the other 8 percent of available business.

The railroads have been the most severely injured of the competitive forms of passenger transportation. It is obvious that the long distance intercity limited passenger train is approaching extinction. The only question now is — when?

The motor bus is likewise declining though not quite as dramatically. Its long-distance patterns are beginning to resemble those of the train.

The airlines seem slated to win the race. They are blessed by superb equipment utilization, which gives them a sound economic base. Their fixed-plant expenses are comparatively negligible.

This prophetic picture by Ansel Adams seems to put all these slowly evolving patterns into a whole.

Ansel Adams photograph
Wells Fargo Bank, San Francisco

Everett L. DeGolyer, Jr. was a well-known book collector, teacher, and railroad buff. Graduated from Princeton University in 1946, he returned to Dallas where he managed the family estate and devoted much time to public service. In 1974 he joined the history faculty at Southern Methodist University and was Director of the DeGolyer Library, which he and his father collected and gave to the university. His interests were reflected in his memberships in the Grolier Club and the Railway and Locomotive Historical Society. He served on the council of the American Antiquarian Society until his death in 1977. THE TRACK GOING BACK was first published in 1969 to accompany an exhibition to commemorate the centennial of the completion of the first transcontinental railroad.